THIS NOTEBOOK BELONGS TO:

Paper Juice

Made in the USA
Columbia, SC
23 February 2020

88298560R00085